D1314128

REASONS TO CARE ABOUT
POLAR BEARS

[Animals in Peril]

Rebecca E. Hirsch

Enslow Publishers, Inc.
40 Industrial Road
Box 398
Berkeley Heights, NJ 07922
USA
http://www.enslow.com

Library of Congress Cataloguing-in-Publication Data
Hirsch, Rebecca E.
  Top 50 reasons to care about polar bears : animals in peril / by Rebecca E. Hirsch.
    p. cm. — (Top 50 reasons to care about endangered animals)
  Includes bibliographical references and index.
  Summary: "Readers will learn about polar bears—their life cycle, diet, young, habitat, and reasons why they
are endangered animals"—Provided by publisher.
  ISBN 978-0-7660-3458-7
  1. Polar bear—Juvenile literature. 2. Endangered species—Juvenile literature. I. Title. II. Title: Top fifty
reasons to care about polar bears.
  QL737.C27H546 2010
  599.786—dc22
                                      2008048693

Printed in the United States of America

092009 Lake Book Manufacturing, Inc., Melrose Park, IL

10 9 8 7 6 5 4 3 2 1

To Our Readers: We have done our best to make sure all Internet Addresses in this book were active and appropriate when we went to press. However, the author and the publisher have no control over and assume no liability for the material available on those Internet sites or on other Web sites they may link to. Any comments or suggestions can be sent by e-mail to comments@enslow.com or to the address on the back cover.

⚙ Enslow Publishers, Inc., is committed to printing our books on recycled paper. The paper in every book contains 10% and 30% post-consumer waste (PCW). The cover board on the outside of each book contains 100% PCW. Our goal is to do our part to help young people and the environment too!

Photographs: Jan Rysavy/iStockphoto, cover inset, 1; Suzi Eszterhas/Nature Picture Library, 1, 51, 52; John Pitcher/iStockphoto, 4, 10, 14, 16, 22, 27, 35, 46, 47, 53, 57, 83, 96, 99; Thomas Pickard/iStockphoto, 6; Ralph Lee Hopkins/National Geographic/Getty Images, 9; David Parsons/iStockphoto, 13; iStockphoto, 19, 63, 79, 82; Paul Tessier/iStockphoto, 18; Nutscode/T Service/Photo Researchers, Inc., 20; James Richey/iStockphoto, 21, 84; Tom Mangelsen/Nature Picture Library, 23, 42, 87; Steven Kazlowski/Nature Picture Library, 24, 37, 45, 54; Eric Baccega/Nature Picture Library, 26, 77; Doug Allan/Nature Picture Library, 28, 38; Sofia Kozlova/iStockphoto, 29; Red Line Editorial, 30; Cindy Haggerty/Shutterstock, 32; Karel Delvoye/iStockphoto, 33; Mats Forsbert/Nature Picture Library, 34; Dawn Nichols/iStockphoto, 41; David Pike/Nature Picture Library, 48, 59; Terry Andrewartha/Nature Picture Library, 56; North Wind Picture Archives, 60; Mike Potts/Nature Picture Library, 64; Photo Library, 67; Lowell Georgia/Corbis, 68; David T. Gomez/iStockphoto, 71; Will Parson/Shutterstock, 72; Markus Schreiber/AP Images, 73; Erlend Kvalsvik/iStockphoto, 74; Sue Flood/Nature Picture Library, 78, 91; Keith Levit/Shutterstock Images, 80; Martha Holmes/Nature Picture Library, 85, 92; Staffan Widstrand/Nature Picture Library, 88; Cindy Creighton/iStockphoto, 94; Tom Vezzo/Nature Picture Library, 95

Cover caption: A polar bear cub peeks over its mother's side.
Suzi Eszterhas/Nature Picture Library

CONTENTS

ENDANGERED POLAR BEARS

Polar bears are among the best-known animals of the Arctic. Since ancient times, people have admired their strength and power. Although the bear is at the top of the Arctic's food chain, it is at risk of extinction.

Human behavior is probably the most important threat to the bears and their habitat. Man-made structures can block polar bears from their hunting and birthing grounds. Hunting, pollution, and oil exploration all add difficulties to a polar bear's daily life.

The Arctic is growing warmer, causing polar sea ice to melt at an alarming rate. Polar bears need sea ice in order to hunt seals.

In 2008, the International Union for Conservation of Nature (IUCN) listed climate change and the resulting loss of sea ice as a threat to polar bears' survival. According to the organization, polar bears risk extinction within one hundred years if the loss of sea ice continues.

Humankind must correct the actions that are hurting polar bears. Through education about polar bears, we will be better able to see how our actions affect these animals. And we can support laws and groups that help polar bears and regulate human activity in the Arctic.

◀ THE POLAR BEAR IS IN DANGER.

GETTING TO KNOW POLAR BEARS

REASON TO CARE # 1

Polar Bears Need Help

No other animal symbolizes the far North like the great white polar bear. To ancient people, it was a cunning hunter and a fearsome enemy, worthy of respect and admiration. To Norse poets, it was "the rider of icebergs" and "the sailor of the floe."[1] To modern people, it is a beloved animal, playful, curious, and clever.

Polar bears are survivors, able to thrive in one of the harshest climates on the planet. But now the Arctic's climate is changing. The icy world to which polar bears are so well suited is shrinking. Unless people act, these great animals may be in danger of disappearing.

[A floe is a wide, flat slab of floating sea ice. Polar bears stand on floes to hunt seals.]

◄ THE POLAR BEAR HAS BEEN KNOWN AS THE "RIDER OF ICEBERGS."

Polar Bears Are
the Only Marine Bears

Although polar bears are sometimes spotted on land, they are far more at home on sea ice. They wander along open cracks in the ice or float on broken slabs of pack ice, always on the lookout for seals to eat. Polar bears also stand on sea ice while hunting. They are so dependent on sea ice that some scientists consider them to be marine animals. That makes them the only marine bears in the world.

[A marine animal is an animal that lives in or depends on the sea. Some other marine animals include whales, seals, penguins, sea gulls, sharks, and sea turtles.]

▶ POLAR BEARS NEED SEA ICE TO HUNT.

REASON TO CARE # 3

Polar Bears Are the Largest Carnivores

The polar bear is one of the most easily identifiable animals on the planet. Its fur looks white. It has black lips, a black nose, a long neck, enormous paws, and a small tail and ears.

Female bears weigh about 330 to 550 pounds (150 to 250 kilograms). Males weigh 775 pounds (350 kilograms) or more. A large male can reach a weight of 1,500 pounds (680 kilograms)—more than the weight of two large Siberian tigers. On its hind legs, a large polar bear might stand 13 feet (4 meters) tall. The polar bear is the largest carnivore on land.

[Polar bear fur is not actually white, but transparent. It looks white because it scatters and reflects light, just as snow and ice do.]

◄ A LARGE POLAR BEAR WEIGHS ABOUT 100 POUNDS MORE THAN TWO SIBERIAN TIGERS ADDED TOGETHER.

Polar Bears
Are Ancient

No one knows just how or when polar bears came into existence. Scientists think that as many as 200,000 years ago, a group of brown bears became stranded in the frozen North. Some of these were dark brown, and others were light brown. The bears survived by hunting seals. The light-colored bears were more likely to survive, because they blended in with the ice and snow. Their camouflage allowed them to sneak up on prey, and so they had better success while hunting.

Over the years, the bears adapted to life in their Arctic home. Eventually, a new species evolved—the great white bear.

[In 2007, a 110,000-year-old jawbone from a polar bear was discovered. It is the oldest polar bear fossil ever found.]

▶ POLAR BEARS HAVE ADAPTED TO ARCTIC LIFE OVER MANY GENERATIONS.

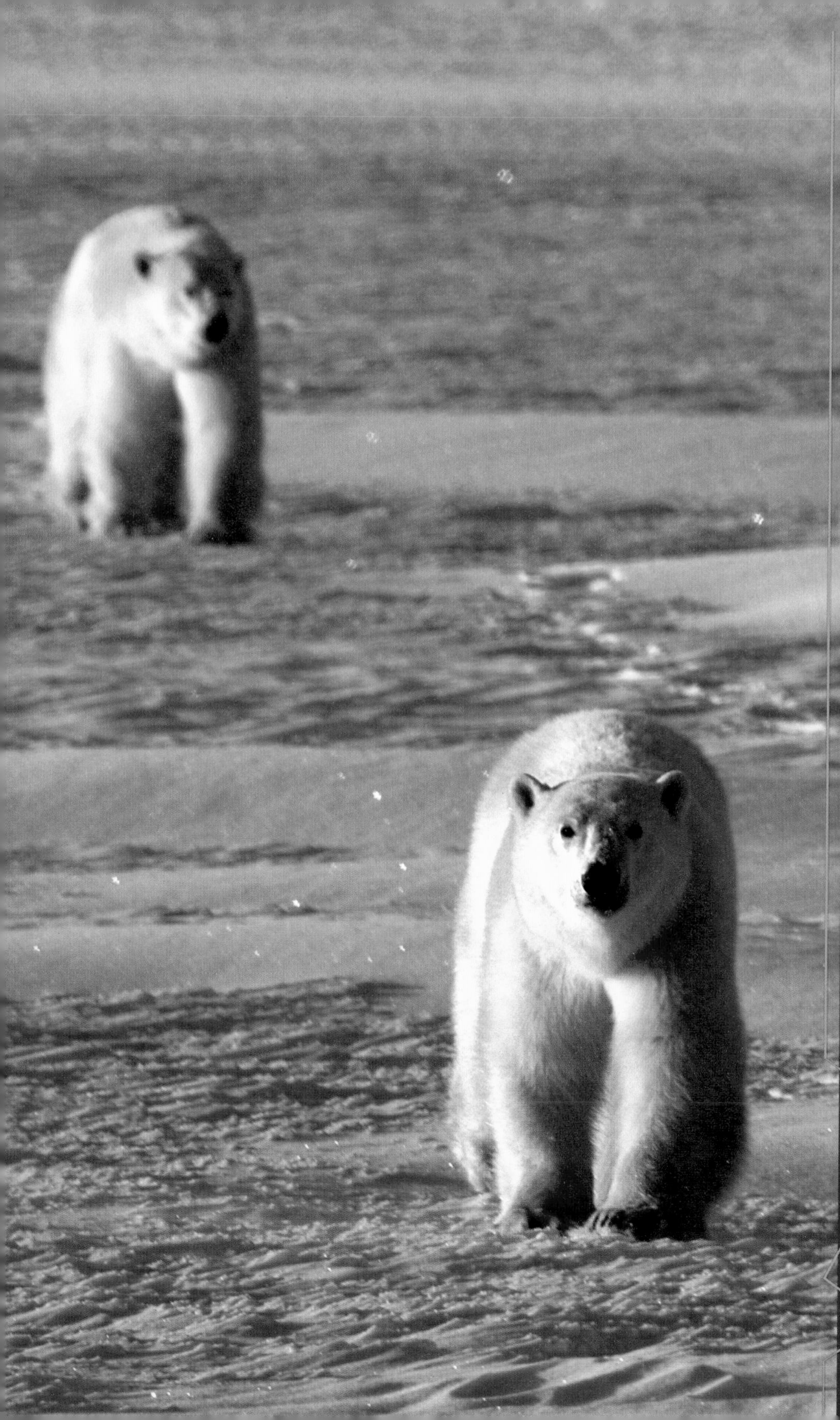

REASON TO CARE # 5
The Arctic Is Changing

Serious challenges threaten the future of polar bears. Climate change is melting the ice that bears need to hunt. Pollution is entering the food chain, increasing the death rate of cubs, who are more vulnerable to toxins. Some people want to drill for oil in the Arctic. However, some conservationists worry that drilling could spell further trouble by bringing bears and humans into contact more often.

No one can say what the future of polar bears will be. Some people believe the bears can adapt to changes to the Arctic in ways we may not expect. But some scientists fear that unless threats to polar bears are removed, the animals could face extinction.

◄ POLAR BEARS FACE NEW CHALLENGES AS THE ARCTIC'S CLIMATE CHANGES.

ARCTIC ADAPTATIONS

REASON TO CARE # 6

Polar Bears Live in Sub-zero Temperatures

Imagine life in the frozen North. In winter, the sun rises briefly or not at all, temperatures can drop to −50 degrees Fahrenheit, and fierce winds fill the air with blinding snow.

During the summer, the northern part of Earth is tilted toward the sun. The days are longer and the nights are shorter. The Arctic faces the sun longer than any other part of the planet. From mid-April to mid-August, the sun does not set. Even so, it is still quite cold.

Food is abundant in some seasons, but there is little to be found in others. Polar bears have adapted to seasons of feasting and famine.

The Arctic is sometimes called "the land of the midnight sun" because the sun does not set during the summer.

POLAR BEARS LIVE IN THE "LAND OF THE MIDNIGHT SUN."

Polar Bears Are
Built for Arctic Life

Polar bears have adaptations for living in the Arctic that their cousins, brown bears, do not.

Brown Bears Have:

1. blunt teeth (grind plants)
2. larger ears and tail
3. smaller paws
4. light or dark brown fur

▼ BROWN BEAR

▲ POLAR BEAR

Polar Bears Have:

5. long neck (helps bears swim)
6. larger paws (grip slippery snow and ice)
7. smaller ears and tail (conserve heat)
8. keen senses (help bears find food)
9. sharp teeth (rip through meat)
10. white-looking fur (blends in with snow and ice)

Polar Bears Stay Warm in the Arctic

Polar bears are designed to keep warm. A plush winter coat and a thick layer of special fat called blubber keep out the cold. Under the fur, the polar bear's skin is black to soak up heat from the sun.

Tiny ears and tail keep in heat; larger ones would get cold. Even the polar bear's large size keeps it warm. A large, rounded body holds heat efficiently.

▼ INFRARED FILM SHOWS THAT POLAR BEARS ARE VERY WELL INSULATED.

▲ A POLAR BEAR'S BLACK NOSE STANDS OUT AGAINST ITS FUR.

REASON TO CARE # 9

Polar Bears Protect Their Noses

Some people believe a polar bear will cover its black nose with its paws while hunting to better blend in with the snow. However, scientists who have spent many hours watching the bears have never observed this.

If a polar bear feels cold, it will curl into a ball and cover its nose with its paws. The nose is less insulated than the rest of the polar bear's body, so covering it helps stop heat loss.

Polar Bears Use
Snow to Stay Warm

The great white bears do not hibernate, but they do have ways of escaping the worst winter weather. When a fierce winter storm hits, a polar bear will dig a small pit in the snow. It then lies down, letting the falling snow cover it. This blanket of snow helps keep the bear's body heat from escaping. The bear then sleeps under the snow. When the storm passes, the animal wakes up, shakes off the snow, and resumes hunting.

▼ POLAR BEARS ESCAPE STORMS BY BURROWING INTO THE SNOW.

▲ POLAR BEARS LOUNGE IN THE SNOW TO COOL OFF.

REASON TO CARE # 11

Polar Bears Know How to Cool Off

Imagine wearing your warmest coat all summer. That is how a polar bear feels on a warm day. Staying cool can sometimes be difficult.

The bears have many strategies to avoid overheating. They walk slowly. If they have to move quickly, they will run only for short distances before walking again. Other ways polar bears cool off are taking a swim, eating snow, and lying on their backs with their feet in the air.

REASON TO CARE # 12

Polar Bears
Are Agile on Ice

Polar bears walk at a slow, plodding pace with their heads bobbing from side to side. But Inuit hunters know not to be fooled by the animals' slow movements. Over short distances, the bears can easily outrun most humans.

[In short bursts, a polar bear can run 25 miles per hour, as fast as a horse.]

A polar bear is sure-footed on ice. The bottoms of its big, furry paws are covered with bumps that keep it from slipping. Large paws, up to 12 inches (30 centimeters) across, spread out the animal's weight so it does not break through thin ice.

[Polar bears crawl across very thin ice to keep from breaking through.]

◄ A POLAR BEAR'S PAWS KEEP IT FROM SLIPPING ON THE ICE.

REASON TO CARE # 13

Polar Bears
Can Swim for Miles

Polar bears are almost as comfortable in water as they are on ice. They often swim more than 60 miles without resting. They paddle with their large, partially webbed forepaws and steer with their hind legs. Their fat helps keep them afloat and their water-repellant fur quickly dries afterward.

▼ POLAR BEARS ARE EXCELLENT SWIMMERS.

▲ POLAR BEARS CAN EASILY SWIM MORE THAN 60 MILES
WITHOUT RESTING.

Sometimes a bear will slip into the water to hunt a seal that is resting on the ice. Gliding through the water with only its black nose sticking up, the bear silently approaches the seal. Then it lunges onto the ice and grabs its prey.

[Although polar bears can manage swims of more than 100 miles at one time, they have been known to drown when they get too far from land.]

Polar Bears Play

Because adult polar bears usually live by themselves, they do not have much need to communicate with other bears. But bears do sometimes send messages to each other by the way they behave.

[Playing is important for polar bear cubs. It helps the baby bears learn key survival skills.]

▼ TWO POLAR BEARS PLAY FIGHTING

▲ POLAR BEARS IN ZOOS PLAY WITH TOYS.

When a polar bear growls, it is telling another bear to stay away from its food. A bear that wags its head from side to side or stands on its hind legs with its paws at its side is telling another bear it wants to play. When polar bears play, it often looks as though they are fighting. However, they are careful not to injure each other.

[Polar bears in zoos play with toys such as plastic floats, buckets, blankets, and "popsicles"—fish and other snacks frozen in blocks of ice.]

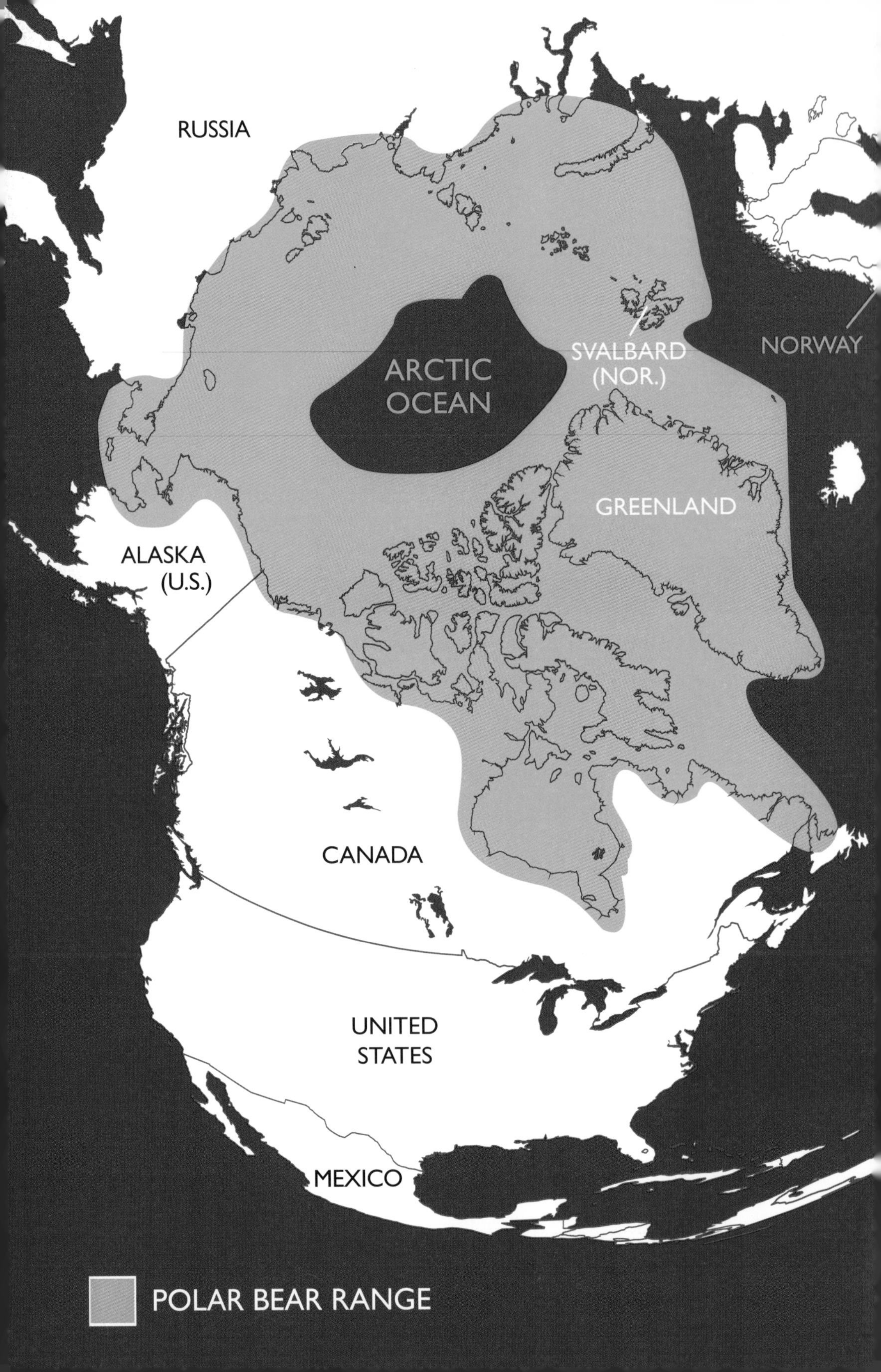

RUSSIA

ARCTIC
OCEAN

SVALBARD
(NOR.)

NORWAY

GREENLAND

ALASKA
(U.S.)

CANADA

UNITED
STATES

MEXICO

POLAR BEAR RANGE

FINDING FOOD

Polar Bears Travel Thousands of Miles

Polar bears live across 5 million square miles of the Arctic. They can be found in Alaska, Canada, Greenland, Norway, and Russia. Mostly they live near the edge of sea ice where they can hunt for seals.

Every polar bear roams within a home range as it looks for prey. A polar bear's range is often very large. It is not unusual for a bear to wander an area the size of South Carolina.

[In their poems, the Inuit call the polar bear *pihoqahiaq*, which means "the ever-wandering one."]

◄ THE POLAR BEAR LIVES THROUGHOUT THE ARCTIC.

REASON TO CARE # 16

Polar Bears Eat Almost Anything

Polar bears eat just about anything they want. They are fearsome predators—the top carnivores in the Arctic. Their only enemies are humans and occasionally other bears.

The polar bear's favorite food, however, is the ringed seal, which live in the Arctic by the millions. The bears also catch and eat young beluga whales, narwhal, walruses, sea birds, geese, and ducks.

▼ THE POLAR BEAR IS THE ARCTIC'S TOP CARNIVORE.

▲ A POLAR BEAR'S FAVORITE FOOD IS RINGED SEAL.

On land, polar bears will eat reindeer, bird eggs, berries, grasses, kelp, whale carcasses, and even humans.

Polar bear attacks on humans are very rare. In all of Canada and Alaska, only eight people have been killed by polar bears in the last thirty years.

[A female bear once killed a white whale, pulled the 2,000-pound whale out of the water, and dragged it 20 feet across the ice.]

Polar Bears
Are Clever Hunters

Like all sea mammals, seals must come up for air. In winter, when ice covers the water, seals use their sharp claws to cut breathing holes in the ice. With its powerful nose, a polar bear will sniff out a breathing hole. The bear will stand on the ice above the hole, patiently waiting for the seal to emerge. When the seal pops its head out of the water, the bear grabs it with its claws. The bear pulls the seal onto the ice and kills it with a bite to the head.

▼ A POLAR BEAR STALKS A SEAL LYING ON THE ICE.

▲ POLAR BEARS GUARD HOLES IN THE ICE, WAITING FOR SEALS TO COME UP TO BREATHE.

Polar bears also stalk seals that bask on the ice. Slow and patient, the bear will carefully place a paw on the snow to keep from making a crunching noise. The seal might raise its head and look around, but the bear, camouflaged against the snow, keeps moving silently closer. At about 20 feet away, the bear speeds across the ice and pounces on the unlucky seal.

[Seals need to come up through the ice to breathe. They can maintain breathing holes through almost 6 feet of ice.]

Polar Bears
Hunt Seals

Seven to eight million ringed seals live in the Arctic. Where ringed seals live, polar bears are likely to be found. The bears are always on the lookout for their favorite prey.

Just as bears have learned to hunt seals, seals have learned the art of escape. Seals swim underwater searching for fish or other food. They come to the surface to breathe every five to fifteen minutes. In winter, when ice forms over the water, seals cut breathing holes in the ice. A seal that cut only one breathing hole probably would have a short life, since it would likely emerge to find a polar bear waiting for it. But seals have learned to outwit bears by cutting several breathing holes. The bears must wait patiently at a breathing hole, not knowing where a seal will emerge for its next breath.

▶ SEALS LIVE THROUGHOUT THE ARCTIC.

Polar Bears
Eat a Lot of Meat

Spring is the season when polar bears fatten up. It is the time when pregnant seals haul themselves out of the water and give birth in dens on the ice. The seal pups, not yet wary of predators, make easy prey for the polar bears.

A seal pup might make a nice snack for a polar bear, but a large ringed seal, weighing 150 pounds and covered with 2 to 3 inches of blubber, makes a solid meal. When food is plentiful, picky bears eat only the skin and blubber. They leave the rest for young bears and other animals to eat.

[A hungry polar bear can eat 150 pounds of blubber at one meal.]

◀ AN AVERAGE RINGED SEAL WEIGHS AROUND 150 POUNDS.

Polar Bears Survive When Food Is Scarce

As spring turns to summer, food becomes difficult for polar bears to find. In summer, the ice retreats far from shore, and in some areas, it melts completely. Without ice, the bears cannot hunt. Bears might swim to sea to find floating pack ice for hunting. In some places, bears go without food as they wait for the ice to return.

When food is scarce, polar bears live off their stored fat and enter a state of "walking hibernation." Even though a bear is still moving around, its metabolism slows down to save energy. When food becomes abundant again, the bear's metabolism revs back up.

▶ POLAR BEARS CAN GO FOR LONG PERIODS OF TIME WITHOUT FOOD.

Polar Bears
Are Clean

Eating seal is a messy business. Dirty, matted fur does not insulate well against the cold, so polar bears wash after every meal.

After eating, a bear will amble over to a pool of water and wash its paws and muzzle. If water isn't available, the bear will rub its head in the snow, push forward on its belly, and roll on its back. Mothers lick their cubs to clean them. They also teach the young bears how to wash themselves in the snow and water.

[Polar bear fur has two layers—a soft underlayer and a long outer layer.]

◄ POLAR BEARS LIKE TO KEEP CLEAN.

Polar Bears Share

Polar bears are mostly solitary creatures, but they sometimes come together around a big source of food. The bear that finds a washed-up whale carcass will sometimes share if other bears come begging.

A begging bear will approach the food slowly, low to the ground. It circles the carcass and meekly touches its nose to the nose of the bear in charge. If the head bear is in a sharing mood, it will let the other bear eat.

[Scientist Lloyd Lowrey once saw polar bears hunting beluga whales that were trapped in a large hole in the ice. A group of bears gathered for a feast. Together, they pulled forty or more whales from the water.]

▶ A GROUP OF POLAR BEARS SHARES A WHALE CARCASS.

REASON TO CARE # 23
Arctic Foxes
Follow Polar Bears

In times of abundance, polar bears will eat only the blubber and skin of a seal, leaving the meat behind. Arctic foxes often follow a bear and eat what is left. Sometimes dozens of foxes can be seen scavenging the leftovers from of a polar bear's meal.

▼ ARCTIC FOXES FOLLOW POLAR BEARS AND EAT THEIR LEFTOVERS.

▲ POLAR BEARS USUALLY TOLERATE FOXES.

Polar bears usually ignore the foxes, though foxes must be careful to keep their distance. Sometimes a fox will nip at a bear's heels, trying to drive the bear from its prey. The bear might get annoyed and lunge or snap at the fox. A hungry bear could turn on a fox and eat it.

RAISING CUBS

REASON TO CARE # 24

Pregnant Polar Bears Gain a Lot of Weight

Polar bears mate in spring, when food is most abundant. The male bear fights off other males to win the attention of a female. The male and female stay together for a week or more.

After mating, the pregnant female continues to hunt, filling up on seals. She is storing the fat she will need to get through the winter. She will need to gain at least 450 pounds to give birth, nurse her cubs, and survive the winter.

◄ POLAR BEARS LIVE OFF STORED FAT WHILE THEY NURSE THEIR CUBS.

Polar Bears Build Their Own Dens

In the fall, while other polar bears stalk the sea ice in search of seals, pregnant females head inland to build a den. Often a female builds her den in the same area where she was born. She digs her den in a hillside or a snow bank.

Each den has a narrow entrance that slopes upward, keeping warm air inside the den. The room inside is only about 6 feet wide, 5 feet long, and 3 feet high. Later, the cubs may dig small rooms off the main one.

[Warmed by body heat, a den can be 40 degrees Fahrenheit warmer than the air outside.]

▶ POLAR BEARS DIG DENS IN HILLSIDES OR IN SNOW BANKS.

Polar Bear Cubs Are Tiny

Sometime around December, mothers give birth to their cubs, often twins. The cubs are born tiny and helpless. Each one weighs about 1 pound (.5 kilograms), about the size of a rat. They are blind, deaf, and nearly hairless.

The mother cuddles her tiny cubs to keep them warm and nourishes them with her rich milk. A mother polar bear's milk contains around 33 percent fat. By comparison, human milk contains only 3 to 5 percent fat.

▼ CUBS ARE FURRY AND CHUBBY BY THE TIME THEY LEAVE THE DEN.

▲ RICH POLAR BEAR MILK HELPS CUBS GROW BIG AND HEALTHY.

The cubs need the fatty milk to survive and grow quickly in the freezing conditions. In spring, the cubs emerge from the den to begin life on the ice. They are furry and weigh 20 pounds (9 kilograms) or more.

REASON TO CARE # 27

Mother Polar Bears Go for Months Without Food

In spring, when the mother bear and her cubs climb out of the den, the mother is thin and hungry. During the four to eight months in her den, the mother went without food or water. She gave birth, nourished her cubs, and kept herself alive entirely off the body fat she stored the previous spring and summer. This long fast is the reason female bears need to put on an astonishing amount of weight—450 pounds—just to give birth to healthy cubs.

[Unlike female polar bears, male polar bears can hunt all year.]

◄ MOTHER POLAR BEARS DON'T EAT UNTIL THEIR CUBS CAN LEAVE THE DEN.

Mother Polar Bears
Teach Cubs to Hunt

As the hungry mother begins to hunt, her cubs obediently tag along. The mother stays close by her cubs, grooming and nuzzling them often. Powerful and protective, she keeps away adult males, who sometimes attack and kill young bears.

▼ CUBS IMITATE THEIR MOTHERS TO LEARN SURVIVAL SKILLS.

▲ POLAR BEARS TEACH THEIR CUBS HOW TO HUNT.

The cubs follow their mother wherever she goes, imitating her as she hunts. But cubs do not have the patience for hunting. They lose interest and start to play. They nip, push, and chase each other, and splash in puddles on the ice.

At age two or older, cubs are ready to leave their mother and go off to hunt on their own. At first, most young bears are not good hunters and must rely on leftovers from other bears' meals.

Only the Strongest Polar Bears Survive

The death rate among cubs is high. For every ten cubs born, six die before reaching adulthood. They are killed by starvation, accidents, or attacks by adult bears. Bears that reach adulthood have learned how to survive in the Arctic.

[Polar bears that reach adulthood usually live fifteen to eighteen years in the wild, although some may live thirty years or more. Bears in zoos live longer. One bear at the Detroit Zoo lived to the age of forty-three.]

At age four or five, a female bear is ready to mate and give birth. She will give birth only every three years, after she has weaned her cubs from the previous litter. A male won't mate until age eight to ten, when he is strong enough to fight off other males.

[Scientists learn the age of a bear by removing a small tooth, slicing the tooth into sections, and counting the rings.]

▶ CUBS MUST LEARN HOW TO SURVIVE IN THE ARCTIC.

POLAR BEARS IN CULTURE

REASON TO CARE # 30

Ancient Cultures Respected the Polar Bear

For thousands of years, polar bears roamed the frozen North without ever seeing a human. Then, several thousand years ago, the first people arrived. They may have walked over the frozen Bering Sea from Asia to Alaska. Or they may have come in boats. No one knows for sure.

Ancient Dorset people made carvings of many of the animals in the North, especially polar bears. Archaeologists have uncovered polar bear masks, carvings, and other artifacts at Dorset campsites. These carvings show that the ancient people admired and feared the great white bears.

[Today, the native people of northern Canada, Greenland, and Alaska are known as Inuit or Eskimo, depending on their specific tribe.]

◀ ARCTIC NATIVES RESPECT THE POLAR BEAR.

Europeans Were Fascinated By Polar Bears

In the nineteenth century, European explorers began arriving in the Arctic. They came from England, Norway, Sweden, Italy, and other countries. Mostly, they came to conquer the Arctic and take gemstones, animal furs, and other treasures. These European explorers were both fascinated by and fearful of the polar bear. Their ship logs tell of countless bears being shot and killed.

[Norse poets praised the polar bear for having "the strength of twelve men and the wit of eleven."[2]]

▶ THIS 1870s ENGRAVING SHOWS EARLY EUROPEAN EXPLORERS ATTACKING POLAR BEARS.

REASON TO CARE # 32

People Used Polar Bears for Survival

Native people of the far North have long used Arctic animals to help them survive. Of all the Arctic's creatures, humans have the fewest cold weather adaptations. Without any protection, a person would die within minutes in the Arctic winter.

Polar bear meat and fat provide native people with the energy they need to survive the cold. Because polar bear fur repels water, they use it to make warm—and waterproof—clothing, blankets, and rugs. In the past, most Inuit clothing was made from sealskins.

In Greenland, it is a sign of status for an Inuit boy to wear polar bear skin pants.

◄ THE MEAT AND SKINS OF POLAR BEARS HELPED ARCTIC PEOPLE SURVIVE.

Polar Bears Inspired Legends

The polar bear is featured in many traditional Inuit legends and stories. Some stories tell of polar bears that were almost human. These talking bears lived in igloos and walked on their hind legs. They could take off their skins once they were alone inside their igloos.

Some Inuit hunters performed special rituals when they killed a polar bear. After a kill, the hunter would hang the bear's skin in his igloo for several days to show respect to the bear's spirit. The hunters believed that if a dead bear was treated with proper respect, the bear would tell other bears, who would allow the hunter to catch them more easily.

Some Inuit hunters would offer the dead bear gifts. They gave males tools such as knives or other weapons. To females, they gave needle cases or hide-scrapers. The hunters believed that the polar bears needed the tools to take with them into the afterlife.

▶ SOME INUIT HUNTERS PERFORMED CEREMONIES AFTER KILLING A POLAR BEAR.

REASON TO CARE # 34

Polar Bear Art Is Beautiful

Indigenous people have long created sculptures of polar bears and other Arctic animals. They carved animal figures onto their weapons as a way to honor and lure the spirits of the animals they hunted.

Today, the polar bear makes its way into other forms of art and popular culture as well. In Canada, both the Northwest Territories and Nunavut issue license plates featuring polar bears. Polar bears decked out in cowboy outfits were the mascots for the 1988 Winter Olympics in Calgary, Canada.

[Indigenous artists usually used walrus tusks to make their carvings, but sometimes they used the tusks of ancient mammoths and mastodons.]

◀ THIS BONE CARVING DEPICTS A HUNTER FIGHTING OFF A POLAR BEAR.

Polar Bears
Have Many Names

Scientists named the polar bear *Ursus martimus*, which means "sea bear." The name was coined in 1774 by a British sea captain. People throughout the Arctic have their own names for the bear:

In Russia, the bear is *beliy medved*, the "white bear."

In Norway and Denmark, the bear is *isbjörn*, the "ice bear."

In Greenland, the bear is *tornassuk*, "the master of helping spirits."

In northern Scandinavia, some people refuse to speak the bear's name, for fear of offending the animal. They instead call it "the old man in the fur cloak."[3]

[One Inuit word for polar bear is *nanook*, or *nanuq*. Nanook is also the nickname of the University of Alaska–Fairbanks sports teams.]

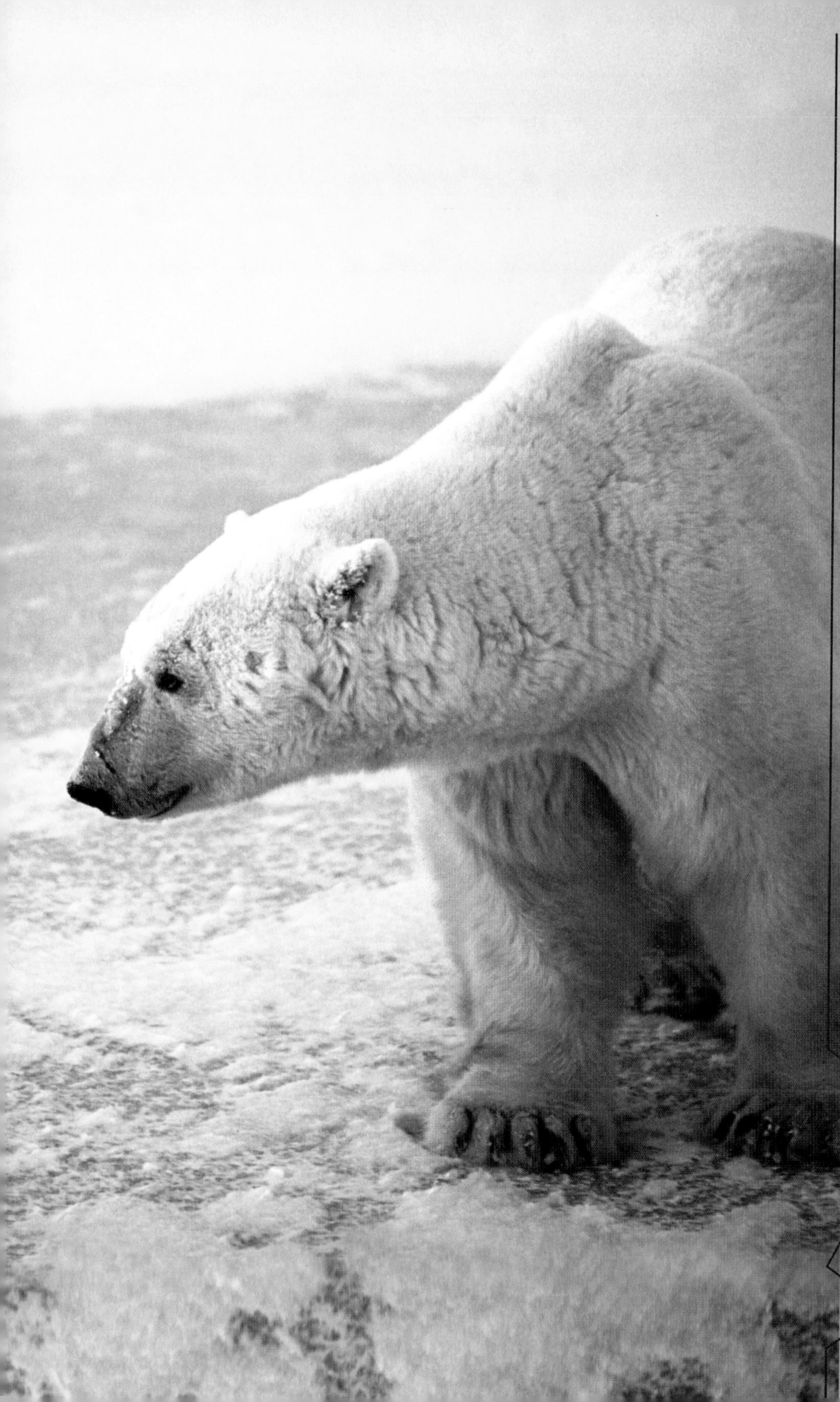

Zoos Teach People About Polar Bears

The only way most people will ever see a polar bear up close is in a zoo. Keeping polar bears in captivity is nothing new. More than two thousand years ago, Ptolemy II, king of ancient Egypt, kept a polar bear in his private zoo. Many zoos today have polar bear exhibits. Crowds of people come to see the bears and know them by name. Clever and playful, polar bears are the stars of the zoo.

▼ CHILDREN WATCH A POLAR BEAR SWIM IN A ZOO.

▲ FAMOUS BABY KNUT FROM THE BERLIN ZOO

People debate whether wild animals should be kept in captivity. Some argue that captivity is not good for wild animals such as polar bears. They believe it is not healthy for a wild animal to be taken from its natural habitat. Others say that zookeepers work together with scientists to give captive bears a good quality of life. They point out that many bears in zoos enjoy state-of-the-art exhibits, complete with waterfalls, chilled pools stocked with fish, and man-made snowdrifts.

One of the most famous zoo bears is Knut, a cub born at the Berlin Zoo in Germany in 2007. After Knut's mother abandoned him, his human keeper raised and bottle-fed him.

THREATS TO POLAR BEARS

REASON TO CARE # 37

Humans Put Polar Bears in Danger

Polar bears have always faced the challenge of surviving in the frozen North. Today, the bears face new challenges, brought about by changes to the Arctic itself. The main threat is climate change, which is causing sea ice to melt. Other dangers include pollution, hunting, and oil drilling.

In 2008, the U.S. government declared polar bears a threatened species under the Endangered Species Act. In addition, the International Union for Conservation of Nature (IUCN) lists polar bears on its Red List of Threatened Species. The IUCN has found that the number of polar bears is likely to decrease in the next thirty-five to fifty years. In some areas, polar bear populations have decreased already.

◀ LOSS OF SEA ICE IS ONE THREAT FACING POLAR BEARS.

Hunting Threatens Polar Bears

Native people still live in the Arctic and tourists go there to seek adventure. When people and polar bears meet, conflict is always a danger. In the past, hunters killed large numbers of polar bears.

In 1973, the International Agreement on the Conservation of Polar Bears was signed. The treaty requires nations to put strict limits on polar bear hunting. Hunting rights are given mainly to native groups. Countries must also protect areas where pregnant bears build their dens. As part of the treaty, scientists come to the frozen land to study the great white bears. They carefully track the number of bears and set limits on how many can be hunted each year.

In most parts of the Arctic, hunting no longer takes a big toll on polar bear populations, and the number of bears has increased in some places. In 2005, scientists estimated that twenty thousand to twenty-five thousand polar bears roamed the North.

▶ TODAY, THERE ARE STRICT LIMITS ON POLAR BEAR HUNTING.

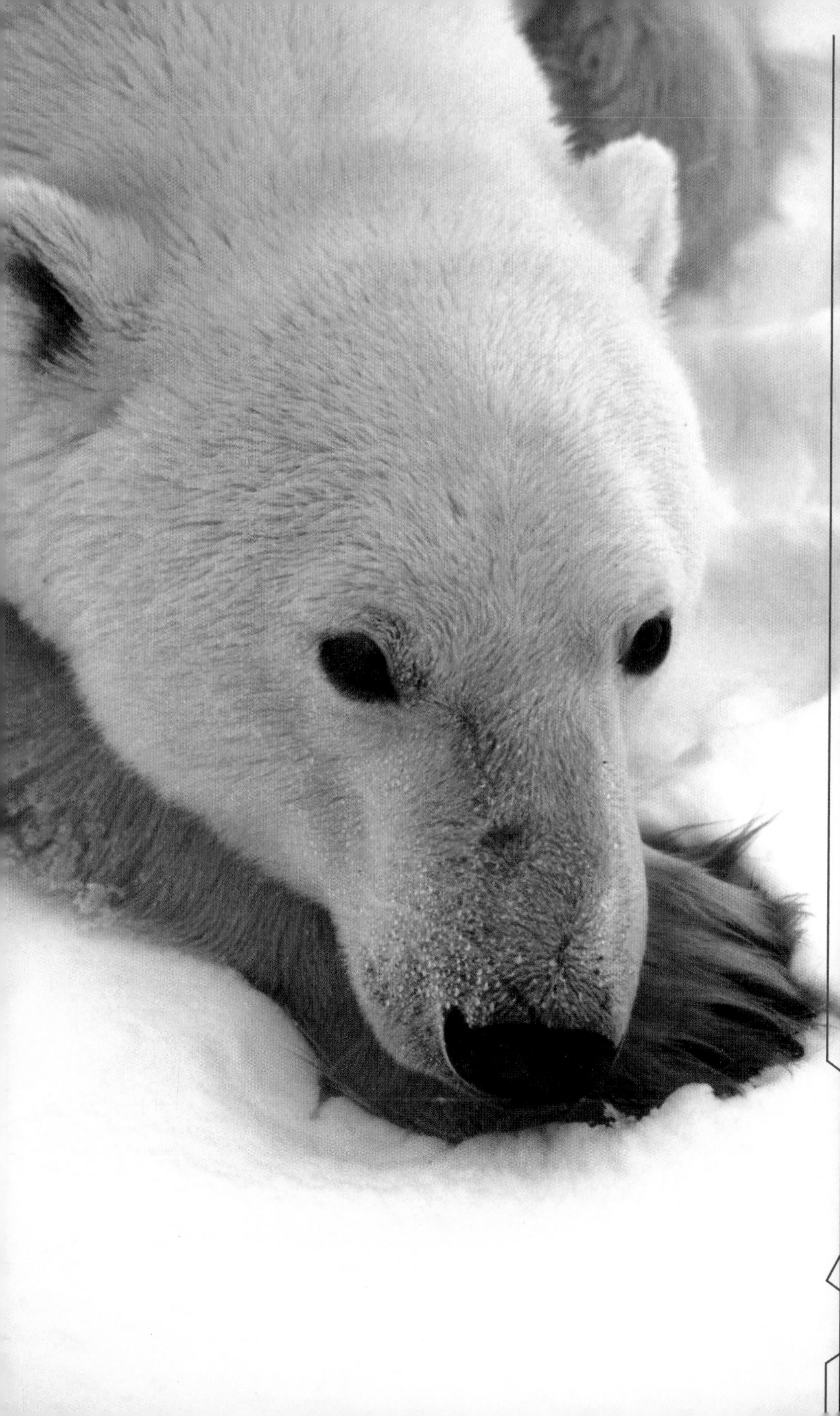

Polar Bears Are Coming to Towns

Signs of bear trouble are cropping up throughout the Arctic. Residents of northern communities report seeing more polar bears close to town. Scientists say the bears are forced inland because the sea ice is melting. Some hungry bears are also attracted to human food and garbage.

Polar bears weigh less and are noticeably skinnier today than they once were. On average, adult males in the Southern Beaufort Sea now weigh 84 pounds less than they did just thirty years ago. And more cubs are dying before reaching adulthood.

▼ SOME POLAR BEARS ARE COMING TOO CLOSE TO TOWNS.

▲ SIGNS WARN PEOPLE TO WATCH OUT FOR POLAR
BEARS IN SPITSBERGEN, NORWAY.

All of these changes are starting to take
their toll on bear populations. The Hudson Bay
area in Canada had 1,200 bears fifteen years ago.
Today, it has fewer than a thousand.

[Historically, polar bear attacks on humans have been rare.
However, as polar bears roam closer to settlements, more
conflicts are inevitable, posing a threat to both humans and
polar bears.]

Chemicals Pollute the Arctic Food Chain

Many people think of the Arctic as spotless land, far removed from the modern world. But everything on the planet is connected. Fumes and chemicals from distant lands are carried to the Arctic by wind, rivers, and ocean streams.

These chemicals make their way into the fat tissues of animals. When one animal eats another, the substances are passed along the food chain. Polar bears, which eat a fat-rich diet and are at the top of the food chain, get a hefty dose of these substances. Mother bears then pass the chemicals to their cubs in their milk.

Evidence suggests that pollution may weaken bears' immune systems, which could make them more likely to get sick. The chemicals also might affect how well bears can reproduce, or they might cause cubs to die young.

◄ POLAR BEARS EAT GARBAGE EVEN THOUGH IT IS UNHEALTHY FOR THEM.

Oil Can Kill
Polar Bears

Humans have long mined the far North for its resources. The Arctic resource that most interests people today is oil. Many people rely on oil to run their cars and heat their homes. Environmental laws hold back Arctic oil drilling in many places, but this could change as the cost of energy increases.

▼ THIS PIPELINE CARRIES OIL ACROSS ALASKA.

▲ HUMANS' DESIRE FOR OIL HAS LED THEM INTO CONFLICT WITH POLAR BEARS.

Mining and drilling can disturb polar bear habitats if not done carefully. These activities also introduce the possibility of an oil spill. During the late 1970s, scientists who were concerned about the effect of oil on polar bears did an experiment. They allowed three polar bears in Churchill, Manitoba, to swim in an oil-covered pool of water. Two of the bears died; the third was taken to a zoo and recovered. The scientists immediately stopped the experiment, but the answer was loud and clear: oil is bad for bears.

Climate Change
Hurts Polar Bears

Most scientists agree that climate change is caused by the burning of oil, natural gas, and coal. Burning these fuels releases carbon dioxide and other gases into the air. The gases trap the heat of the sun, causing the atmosphere to heat up.

The far North has already warmed 4 to 7 degrees Fahrenheit in the past fifty years. Many scientists predict the region will continue to warm and the ice will continue to melt.

▼ CLIMATE CHANGE IS ONE MAJOR THREAT TO POLAR BEARS.

▲ POLAR BEARS SWIM LONG DISTANCES TO REACH THE SEA ICE.

REASON TO CARE # 43

Sea Ice
Is Shrinking

In the far North, the sea ice is shrinking and growing thinner. In places where the summertime distance between ice and land used to be 60 miles, it may now be 120 miles or more.

In some parts of the bears' range, the ice now melts three weeks earlier each summer than it did thirty years ago. That gives the bears less time to hunt. It forces them to go longer without food. Every week that a bear goes without food, it loses 20 pounds.

REASON TO CARE # 44

Arctic Changes
Are Harmful

Of all the changes to the Arctic, the one that threatens polar bears the most is climate change. If sea ice continues to melt, as scientists say it will, the bears will be headed for hard times. Bears are not the only species impacted by climate change. Seals depend on sea ice just as polar bears do. Pregnant seals give birth to their pups in lairs on the ice. When the ice melts too soon, they may be forced to give birth in open water instead. In 2002, several hundred pups drowned because of this.

The Inuit also are affected by changes to the Arctic. Inuit say the signs of warming are everywhere. They are concerned that if polar bear numbers decline, hunting will be outlawed. In that case, they would lose a tradition that has been part of their way of life for thousands of years.

[In 2004, four bears drowned off the coast of Alaska as they tried to swim the growing distance between land and ice.]

▶ MELTING ICE THREATENS MANY ARCTIC ANIMALS.

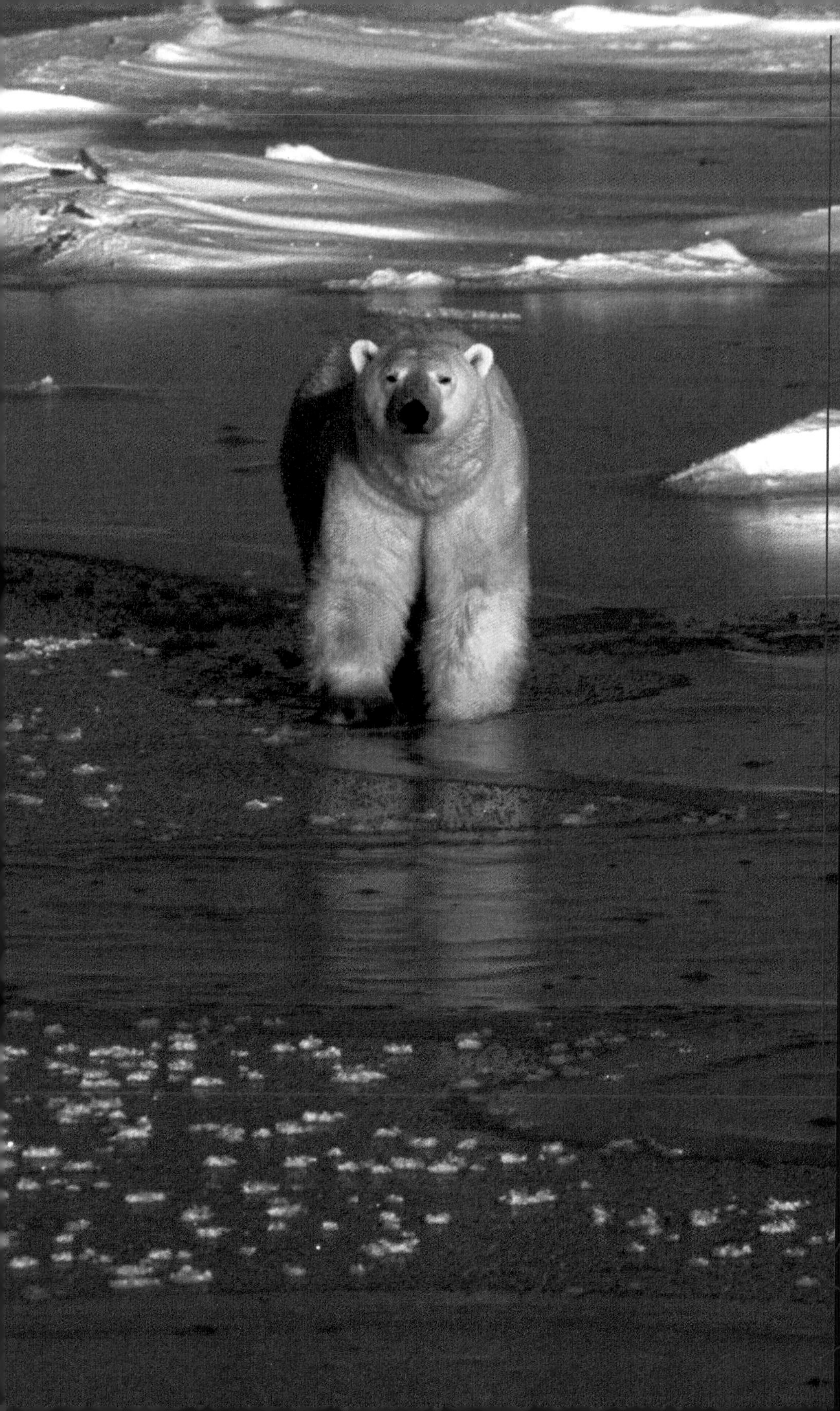

POLAR BEAR CONSERVATION

REASON TO CARE # 45

Hunting Laws
Can Help Polar Bears

In the 1950s and 1960s, hunting was the main threat to polar bears. No one knew how many polar bears were killed by hunters, but experts agreed that excessive hunting was a growing problem.

In 1973, leaders from five nations—Canada, Denmark, Norway, the United States, and the former Soviet Union—prepared the International Agreement on the Conservation of Polar Bears. The nations agreed to protect places where females denned and to restrict hunting. After this, bear populations rebounded in some places.

Today, scientists closely monitor the number of bears and set strict limits on hunting. The good news is that of all the dangers to polar bears, hunting is the easiest to control.

◀ INUIT ARE ALLOWED TO HUNT POLAR BEARS AS PART OF THEIR TRADITIONAL LIFESTYLE.

Scientists Track Polar Bears

Polar bear scientists are learning all they can about this threatened species. One way scientists study the animals is by tagging them.

First, scientists search for bears via helicopter. When a bear is spotted, a scientist shoots it with a harmless drug that temporarily stops the bear from moving. The bear is weighed and measured, tagged, and fitted with a radio collar. The collar sends a signal back to the scientists, which lets them track the bear's movements. This allows scientists to study the bear from very far away. By tracking tagged bears, researchers can learn how long bears live, how many cubs they have, and where they roam.

▶ SCIENTISTS CAN STUDY POLAR BEARS BY TAGGING AND TRACKING THEM.

REASON TO CARE # 47

Inuit Hunters
Understand Polar Bears

Inuit have lived in the Arctic for centuries. They are quick to notice changes to their frozen homeland.

Scientists value Inuit knowledge and understanding of the Arctic. Inuit want to help save the polar bears, so they share with scientists what they know. They teach scientists about the Arctic's seasons and tell them about the changes they observe.

Scientists have provided the Inuit with scientific instruments so they can help monitor changes to the Arctic's weather. Some Inuit hunters accompany scientists onto the sea ice and have learned how to immobilize and tag bears.

[On tagging expeditions, many experienced Inuit hunters are cautious when approaching an immobilized bear. Under normal circumstances, they wouldn't think of going near a large bear that is lying on the ice and breathing normally with its eyes open.]

◀ INUIT HUNTERS AND SCIENTISTS WORK TOGETHER TO SAVE POLAR BEARS.

People Travel to See Polar Bears

The small Canadian town of Churchill, Manitoba, calls itself the Polar Bear Capital of the World. Every fall, when the ice in nearby Hudson Bay melts, bears come ashore to wait for the ice to return. Many tourists, photographers, and bear lovers come to see the animals. Scientists say Churchill is one of the best places in the world to learn about polar bears. More studies have been carried out on Churchill's bears than on any other polar bears.

▼ A MOBILE LODGE TAKES CHURCHILL TOURISTS TO SEE POLAR BEARS.

▲ CHURCHILL IS KNOWN AS "THE POLAR BEAR CAPITAL OF THE WORLD."

What makes Churchill such a great place to study polar bears? For one thing, the town is easy to reach. It is also a lot warmer than other places polar bears live. And the bears live close together, so scientists do not have to spend a lot of time searching for them over miles of ice and snow.

REASON TO CARE # 49

Polar Bear Specialists Can Help

Every few years, the world's top polar bear scientists come together to discuss how to conserve the bears. The tradition began in 1965 with a meeting in Fairbanks, Alaska. It was the first scientific meeting devoted to the conservation of a single species.

That first group of scientists is now the Polar Bear Specialist Group. As of 2008, the Polar Bear Specialist Group had nineteen members, all scientists from the five polar bear nations. These nations are Canada, Denmark (on behalf of Greenland), Norway, Russia, and the United States. The group reviews the status of the bears, sets new limits for hunting, and discusses ideas for protecting them. The Specialist Group has helped put an end to overhunting and has worked to alert the public and lawmakers about other threats to bears.

Since the U.S. government has listed polar bears as a threatened species, the Specialist Group is working even harder. Polar bears may be rugged, but they will only survive with human intervention.

◀ THE POLAR BEAR SPECIALIST GROUP WORKS TO HELP THE FAMOUS ANIMAL.

You Can Help Save Polar Bears

Fun and Rewarding Ways to Help Save Polar Bears

- Read books and articles to learn more about polar bears.
- Visit zoos to see polar bears up close.
- Walk or ride a bike instead of driving. Fumes from cars and trucks contribute to climate change.
- Recycle aluminum cans, glass bottles, plastic, and cardboard.
- Turn off the lights and your television, computer, and other electronics when you are not using them.
- Plant a tree. Trees soak up carbon dioxide from the air.
- Write to your representatives in Congress and ask them to support laws that fight climate change and protect the polar bear's habitat.
- Have your class plan a fund-raiser to support an organization that protects polar bears.

▶ YOU CAN HELP SAVE THE POLAR BEAR!

GLOSSARY

adapt—To change to meet the demands of the environment.

Arctic—The frozen area around the North Pole.

atmosphere—The layer of air that surrounds Earth.

blubber—A thick layer of fat that insulates animals.

camouflage—A way of hiding or blending into the background.

captivity—Being in a zoo instead of the wild.

carbon dioxide—A heat-trapping gas given off when fossil fuels are burned.

carnivore—An animal that eats meat.

conservation—The protection of nature and animals.

endangered—At risk of becoming extinct.

environment—The natural world; the area in which a person or animal lives.

evolve—To change slowly over time.

extinct—Died out completely.

fossil fuel—A fuel, such as oil, coal, or natural gas, that is made of ancient plants and animals.

habitat—The place in which an animal lives; the features of that place including plants, landforms, and weather.

indigenous—Having to do with people who have lived in a place for thousands of years.

insulate—To protect something from losing heat.

Inuit—Indigenous people of the Arctic, formerly known as Eskimos.

metabolism—All of the chemical changes inside an animal's body that convert food to energy.

pack ice—Large broken pieces of floating ice.

pollution—Substances in the air and water that harm the environment and animals that live there.

population—The total number of a group of animals.

range—The entire area in which a species lives; the territory of an individual animal or group of animals.

sea ice—Ice formed when the ocean freezes.

species—A specific group of animals with shared physical characteristics and genes; members within a species can breed with each other to produce offspring.

FURTHER READING

Books

Osborne, Mary Pope. *Polar Bears and the Arctic*. New York: Random House, 2007.

Rosing, Norbert. *Face to Face With Polar Bears*. Washington, DC: National Geographic, 2007.

Rosing, Norbert. *The World of the Polar Bear*. Richmond Hill, ON: Firefly Books, 2006.

Internet Addresses

Anthropolis: Arctic Entertainment and Education
<http://www.athropolis.com/>

San Diego Zoo's Animal Bytes: Polar Bears
<http://www.sandiegozoo.org/animalbytes/t-polar_bear.html>

WWF: Canon Polar Bear Tracker
<http://www.panda.org/polarbears>

SOURCE NOTES

Source Notes

1. "Bear Facts: Name that Bear," *Polar Bears International*, n.d., <http://www.polarbearsinternational.org/ bear-facts/name-that-bear/> (April 5, 2008).
2. Ibid.
3. Ibid.

INDEX